THE STUDENT-PARENTS JOURNEY

(THE LIVED EXPERIENCES OF STUDENT-PARENTS)

THE STUDENT-PARENTS JOURNEY

(THE LIVED EXPERIENCES OF STUDENT-PARENTS)

Sunshine M. Salenga-Talavera,Ph.D.

Alexandra Pasaron

GALDA VERLAG 2025

Bibliografische Information der Deutschen Nationalbibliothek
Die Deutsche Nationalbibliothek verzeichnet diese Publikation in der Deutschen Nationalbibliografie; detaillierte bibliografische Daten sind im Internet über
https://dnb.de abrufbar.

In partial fulfilment for the
Research Class
Bataan Peninsula State University
Dinalupihan Campus

Research in Education

ISBN 978-3-96203-424-5 (Print)
ISBN 978-3-96203-425-2 (E-Book)

TABLE OF CONTENTS

Abstract   i

*"At the End of the Day, the Most
Overwhelming Key to a Child's Success
Is the Positive Involvement of Parents."*
Jane D Hull, Governor of Arizona (1997 to 2003)   1

*"The Way You See People Is the Way
You Treat Them, and the Way You Treat
Them Is What They Become."*
Goethe, a German writer and statesman   7

    Student-Parents: Who are they?   11

    Assistance for the Student-Parents   16

    Challenges among Student-Parent   20

    Education and Student-Parents   22

    Success among Student-Parents   23

    Assistance from Institutions   25

"It's Not What You Look At That Matters. It's What You See."

Henry David Thoreau, essayist, and poet   31

Part I: Lived Experiences of the student-parents through their challenges and Privileges   31

Self-Reliance is a Must   31

Bounded by Time, by Responsibilities   35

The Beam of Balance: Tool for Success   40

So that Others May Learn from It   42

Education begets Education   44

Opportunities to Graduate and Become Professional   47

"Let Us Remember: One Book, One Pen, One Child, and One Teacher Can Change the World."

Malala Yousafzai, Pakistani activist for Education   51

Part I: Lived Experiences of the student-parents through their challenges and Privileges   51

Self-Reliance is a Must   51

Bounded by Time, by Responsibilities   52

The Beam of Balance: Tool for Success   53

Conclusions   55

Recommendations   55

References   57

ABSTRACT

This study was focused only on the lived experiences of student parents as perceived by the students of Bataan Peninsula State University S.Y 2022-2023. It involved the challenges and privileges they are experiencing. There were 5 respondents who had dependent children and has special stories to tell (included and revealed in the chapter 4). Moreover, this study sought to know how student parents deal with their responsibilities of being a parent and also a student. This study includes the narrative inquiry qualitative approach as research design and has output of infographic material in a form of a video to highlight the challenges and privileges of the participants.

Keywords: Lived Experiences, Student-Parents, Challenges, Privileges.

> *"AT THE END OF THE DAY, THE MOST OVERWHELMING KEY TO A CHILD'S SUCCESS IS THE POSITIVE INVOLVEMENT OF PARENTS."*

Jane D Hull, Governor of Arizona (1997 to 2003)

A "Student-Parent" is a parent who is currently enrolled in school and has dependent children. They are accountable for both student and parenting responsibilities, which may put them under pressure to juggle several responsibilities. Coronel, B. (2020b).

The obstacle in the life of student-parents has created changes and challenges. Many parents who have children stop studying because of the consequence that there is no going to be left for their children, according to a recent review by the Institute for Women's Policy Research (2014).

A large portion of women who get pregnant in college end up dropping out temporarily or permanently. Some student parents continue studying because someone will take care of their children, and even though they already know that it is difficult to keep up with study and the responsibility of being a parent, they continue to study to achieve their ambitions and needs. Although one in five college students are parents, undergraduate student parents remain one of the most "invisible" groups in higher education, despite their considerable need for support (Miller, 2019; Reichlin et al. et al., 2019).

Key factors such as a reluctance to self-identify, institutional assumptions of student demographics, and a definitive focus on typically aged students living on or near campus all lead to this population being under-identified and underserved, particularly at four-year universities. Undergraduate college students who are parents represent one in five college students. Compared to non-parents, they are more likely to be: Women; People of color; Older; First-generation college students; Of lower socioeconomic backgrounds (Goodman & Reddy, 2019).

Undergraduate student parents have fewer financial resources and report struggling more financially compared to undergraduate students who are not parents (Goodman & Reddy, 2019; Miller, 2019; Reichlin et al. et al., 2019; GAO, 2019). Student parents report that accessible and affordable child care is their most crucial need (Goodman & Reddy, 2019). While the need for childcare access and funding is critical, there is evidence for other key factors to student parent success, such as case management for academic, housing, and parenting support and a community of like peers. Undergraduate student parents take longer to finish school and are less likely to graduate compared to "traditional" students who are not parents (Ascend at the Aspen Institute, 2019; Zarifa D. et al., 2018).

Within six years, only one-third of undergraduate student parents graduate from college (Miller, 2019). Fifty-two percent of undergraduate student parents drop out of college within six years of enrolling, compared with 32% of non-parents (GAO, 2019). Student parents may be less likely to graduate on time or remain enrolled in classes, yet past research suggests that undergraduate student parents have higher GPAs compared to non-parent students (Reichlin et al. et al., 2019). Previous research also suggests that despite the challenges student parents face, as a group, they are extremely motivated to succeed academically (Goodman & Reddy, 2019). Student parents, particularly single mothers, are motivated by the well-documented positive intergenerational benefits – short-term and long-term – that their pursuit of higher education will have on their children (Goodman & Reddy, 2019). Educated mothers are more likely to create high-quality home learning environments for children and utilize parenting strategies that incorporate learning, as well as serve as role models for higher education achievement (Magnuson, 2007; Monoghan, 2016). Additionally, the monetary returns of a parental college education may lead to more stable home environments and an increased ability to invest in the academic activities of their children (Monoghan, 2016).

Children of educated mothers have improved cognitive development, higher test scores, and better academic outcomes compared to children of mothers with high school degrees or less (Magnuson, 2007). Mothers with college degrees are also more likely to invest in child health-promoting behaviors, which may be why children of more educated mothers have improved health outcomes (Prickett & Augustine, 2016). As adults, children with educated mothers are more likely to graduate from high school, attend college, and graduate from college themselves (Monoghan, 2016). This leads to increased wages and creates an intergenerational cycle of family economic security (Reichlin Cruse, Holtzman, et al., 2019; Reichlin Cruse, Milli et al., 2019).

In light of these challenges facing undergraduate student parents, previous research has delineated key institutional practices that support student parents' needs (Goodman & Reddy, 2019).

Evidence shows that investment in supportive services for student parents leads to a strong return on investment. Improving undergraduate student parents' outcomes is a critical component in college and universities' efforts to promote equity in education access and outcomes (Reichlin Cruse, Holtzman, et al., 2019). In order to improve outcomes (such as graduation, retention, and GPA) for this diverse group of traditionally underrepresented students, higher education institutions need to understand what evidence-based practices exist to address their needs as parents (Pendelton and Atella, 2020).

The main research question of the present study is: What are the Challenges and privileges that student parents have experienced? Exploring the difficulties that student-parents face as a result of the several identities for which they are accountable helps us to understand the Challenges and Privileges they experience.

> ## "THE WAY YOU SEE PEOPLE IS THE WAY YOU TREAT THEM, AND THE WAY YOU TREAT THEM IS WHAT THEY BECOME."

Goethe, a German writer and statesman

In this chapter, the theories relevant, as well as the related literature and studies, are presented on this part.

There are the following theories and approaches used in this study, such as positive parenting, attachment theory, and Child Guidance.

Positive parenting is focused on the understanding that children come into the world primed with the tools and capacities to follow a path of optimal growth and development. This outlook is drawn from positive psychology, which is the study of how people flourish. This movement in the field of psychology arose to counteract the heavily present disease/illness model of human functioning and to focus on what goes right.

It is based on the view that all individuals want to have lives that are meaningful and fulfilling by exploring, enhancing, and using individual strengths and being able to enjoy love, play, and work. Keyes and Haidt identify four hallmark behaviors that express what is needed for people to flourish:

1) Being resilient - the ability to meet the challenges of life and use setbacks and adversity as learning and growing experiences by relying on oneself and having a positive attitude.

2) Able to engage and relate to others.

3) Finding fulfillment through being productive and creative.

4) Looking past ourselves to help others flourish, as well. These are all connected and visible in the study.

Another is the Attachment Theory. Establishing a close parent-child relationship with secure attachment is a hallmark of positive parenting. Attachment theory has a very long and well-researched basis. It is most notably from the work of John Bowlby and Mary Ainsworth, who established the theory beginning in the 1950s. Attachment is particularly important in the area of social and emotional outcomes for children. Fundamentally, the purpose of attachment is so a child feels safe, secure, and protected. Three main types of attachment relationships have been identified. One of the most important determinants of the quality of the attachment relationship is how the parent responds when the child has a need, such as feeling insecure, upset, or afraid.

It's useful to know the need for attachment is so strong in infants and young children that it's not whether they are attached but how healthy that attachment is. Also, children can have any of the types of attachments discussed below with any number of main caregivers. So they could have one for mother, a different with father, and another with a nanny or grandparent.

Secure attachment is most likely to result when parents respond to the child's needs in a way that is sensitive and loving; for instance, they pick the child up when they're crying -- especially in infancy -- speak soothingly, listen to the child. Children then know they can express such feelings and will get comfort.

Their strategy for using their parent to manage their distress is to find and stay close. When a young child has a secure attachment, they can use their parent (or primary caregiver) as a base from which to explore, but yet feel they can get reassurance and comfort if needed.

Lastly, the **Child Guidance**. The work of Rudolf Dreikurs is frequently cited as a major influence on positive parenting. His work is an extension of Alfred Adler's Individual Psychology approach, which takes into account the environment of the person in understanding them. Dreikurs' advice on parents guiding the child has a number of components. Among these are: There should be *mutual respect* between a parent and child based on the basic human right of equality. Parents should show encouragement for their child›s efforts, as this indicates they believe in the child and accept them as they are. At the same time, parents should not set standards the child cannot reach, as this will discourage them. Rather than rewards and punishment, parents should *use natural consequences* that stem from the child's actions, as opposed to the parent using their authority to get the child to do or not do something. When disciplining, more acting and less talking, which can lead to arguments, is recommended. Related is for the parent to withdraw by ignoring or leaving the room to remove an audience for the child's attempts at a power struggle. However, this is not the same as withdrawing from the child, just from the conflict. Please note these ideas are not for when a child is in immediate danger or too young to be left alone. Children need to be **taught important skills and habits,** but this should be done when the child is calm and also not when there are others around who aren't in the immediate family, so the child is not too self-conscious. Parents must let children do for themselves when and what they can and accept a child's perhaps still-inadequate efforts if it still gets the job done. They must resist the urge to make it just a bit better or to validate their importance as parents. positive parenting has a rich and solid foundation. Each of these influences provides important elements to help parents provide the best childrearing environment possible. This allows their children to have the best opportunity for optimal development.

Student-Parents: Who are they?

Student-parents' success may be defined in terms of the ability to provide for their family in conjunction with their Education as opposed to solely merit-based academic achievement. This definition reflects what success means for student-parents throughout the paper. Dominant sociological theories suggest that individuals should earn a college degree to provide for their children. Yet, accessing successful support programs for student-parents is challenging because of institutional obstacles such as a lack of childcare and welfare requirements. They are thus not beneficial unless the services can be accessed by all student-parents, regardless of their socioeconomic background.

A "Student-Parent" is a parent who is currently enrolled in school and has dependent children. They are accountable for both student and parenting responsibilities, which may put them under pressure to juggle several responsibilities. Coronel, B. (2020b).

The obstacle in the life of student-parents has created changes and challenges. Many of the parents who have children stop studying because of the consequence that there is no going to be left for their children. According to a recent review by the Institute for Women's Policy Research (2014).

A large portion of women who get pregnant in college end up dropping out temporarily or permanently. Some student parents continue studying because someone will take care of their children, and even though they already know that it is difficult to keep up with study and the responsibility of being a parent, they continue to study to achieve their ambitions and needs.

Although one in five college students are parents, undergraduate student parents remain one of the most "invisible" groups in higher education, despite their considerable need for support (Miller, 2019; Reichlin Cruse, Holtzman, et al., 2019).

Key factors such as a reluctance to self-identify, institutional assumptions of student demographics, and a definitive focus on typically aged students living on or near campus all lead to this population being under-identified and underserved, particularly at four-year universities. Undergraduate college students who are parents represent one in five college students. Compared to non-parents, they are more likely to be: Women; People of color; Older; First-generation college students; Of lower socioeconomic backgrounds (Goodman & Reddy, 2019).

Undergraduate student parents have fewer financial resources and report struggling more financially compared to undergraduate students who are not parents (Goodman & Reddy, 2019; Miller, 2019; Reichlin Cruse, Holtzmann, et al., 2019; GAO, 2019). Student parents report that accessible and affordable child care is their most crucial need (Goodman & Reddy, 2019). While the need for childcare access and funding is critical, there is evidence for other key factors to student parent success, such as case management for academic, housing, and parenting support and a community of like peers. Undergraduate student parents take longer to finish school and are less likely to graduate compared to "traditional" students who are not parents (Ascend at the Aspen Institute, 2019; Zarifa D. et al., 2018).

Within six years, only one-third of undergraduate student parents graduate from college (Miller, 2019). Fifty-two percent of undergraduate student parents drop out of college within six years of enrolling, compared with 32% of non-parents (GAO, 2019). Student parents may be less likely to graduate on time or remain enrolled in classes, yet past research suggests that undergraduate student parents have higher GPAs compared to non-parent students (Reichlin Cruse, Holtzman, et al., 2019). Previous research also suggests that despite the challenges student parents face, as a group, they are extremely motivated to succeed academically (Goodman & Reddy, 2019). Student parents, particularly single mothers, are motivated by the well-documented positive intergenerational benefits – short-term and long-term – that their pursuit of higher education will have on their children (Goodman & Reddy, 2019). Educated mothers are more likely to create high-quality home learning environments for children and utilize parenting strategies that incorporate learning, as well as serve as role models for higher education achievement (Magnuson, 2007; Monoghan, 2016). Additionally, the monetary returns of a parental college education may lead to more stable home environments and an increased ability to invest in the academic activities of their children (Monoghan, 2016).

Children of educated mothers have improved cognitive development, higher test scores, and better academic outcomes compared to children of mothers with high school degrees or less (Magnuson, 2007). Mothers with college degrees are also more likely to invest in child health-promoting behaviors, which may be why children of more educated mothers have improved health outcomes (Prickett & Augustine, 2016). As adults, children with educated mothers are more likely to graduate from high school, attend college, and graduate from college themselves (Monoghan, 2016). This leads to increased wages and creates an intergenerational cycle of family economic security (Reichlin Cruse, Holtzman, et al., 2019; Reichlin Cruse, Milli et al., 2019).

In light of these challenges facing undergraduate student parents, previous research has delineated key institutional practices that support student parents' needs (Goodman & Reddy, 2019).

Evidence shows that investment in supportive services for student parents leads to a strong return on investment. Improving undergraduate student parents' outcomes is a critical component in college and universities' efforts to promote equity in education access and outcomes (Reichlin Cruse, Holtzman, et al., 2019). In order to improve outcomes (such as graduation, retention, and GPA) for this diverse group of traditionally underrepresented students, higher education institutions need to understand what evidence-based practices exist to address their needs as parents (Pendelton and Atella, 2020).

Assistance for the Student-Parents

Although many community college campuses have student-parent support programs, some student participation requirements create barriers that ultimately prevent them from graduating. Studies show how welfare programs such as California Work Opportunities and Responsibility to Kids (CalWORKs), which provides cash aid to student-parents, both negatively and positively affect their academic performance in different ways. However, the evidence regarding the influence that welfare programs have on academic performance is conflicting and thus largely inconclusive. Sandra Austin's study on college persistence among single mothers suggests that low-income parents attending public universities face difficulty fulfilling the academic requirements tied to welfare eligibility, particularly good grades and employment (Austin, 2013).

Findings suggest that the primary reason low-income parents do not continue their higher education is due to the criteria instituted in federally-funded welfare programs. The welfare program previously mentioned, known as both Transitional Assistance for Needy Families (TANF) and CalWORKs, allows low-income parents to receive cash aid for up to four years if they maintain their student enrollment status and work at least 20 hours per week. The required time commitment negatively impacts academic performance and thus acts as a barrier for parents; parents must comply with the programs' requirements to receive and perpetuate their financial aid, yet the requirements become a significant obstacle to achieving those very academic outcomes meant to help them support their families (Austin, 2003, p.100).

Working to fulfill welfare requirements while attending college also creates collateral damage to the family unit. The long hours required to participate in both work and school and the stress involved in juggling such responsibilities can contribute to the neglect of young children. Furthermore, wages from this work combined with financial aid may not even be enough to cover living expenses for single parents and their children. Due to the fear of housing insecurity, many of these students withdraw from college altogether in order to work full-time and be able to Brenda Coronel afford a better living situation. With all of these factors, work and enrollment requirements for federal assistance allow student parents neither academic nor financial stability.

However, in other studies of student-parents, CalWORKs recipients who were parents achieved higher grades than students without children (Fenster, 2004). Judy Fenster, who measures academic success by grades and the number of times each student made the Dean's List, argued that welfare requirements do not act as a barrier to academic performance but rather improve grades by motivating students so they can continue to receive temporary cash aid assistance (2004). Of the 106 students who participated in Fenster's study, 81 (76%) of students did not identify as a parent or welfare recipient, and 25 (24%) identified as a student parent welfare recipient (2004, p.424). The findings showed that parents receiving cash aid earned higher grades and achieved the Dean's List more often than students who did not identify as a parent. Fenster's research suggests that the CalWORKs program provides an effective support system that gives low-income student-parents proper resources to succeed academically. Her findings also suggest that if students are given the resources and choose to utilize support systems, graduation rates will improve (Fenster, 2004).

Building on the findings of previous scholarship, my study will focus on the mental health of student-parents, as well as their identities as parents and racial minorities. Scholars have identified student-parents as feeling at odds with their academic institution, such as feeling isolated and even feeling threatened (Austin, 2013, p. 95). As a result of negative encounters at school, student-parents were less likely to become more involved in academia because they did not feel that they belonged to an academic institution.

According to Claude Steele's study, anxiety results from stereotype threats about minority students, such as student-parents, and when students became aware of existing stereotypes, they tended to perform more poorly on exams and in coursework (1997). In the previous studies mentioned, the grades of student-parents were a primary factor in determining educational success, but researchers did not address the mental state of student-parents. The adverse effects of discrimination against pregnant students and student-parents can impact their mental health and overall academic performance (Ling, 2001, p. 2408). Unlike the previous studies that focused on the academic performance of student-parents, new research has focused on their mental health. The findings from Tamera Ling's study on pregnant and parenting students suggest that stress rose when parents felt stigmatized as incapable of academic success.

Challenges among Student-Parent

The factor of stress explains why a large number of student-parents have dropped out of school. The study from Virginia Brown on student-parents on campus suggests that a population of student-parents experienced stress when attempting to balance school and work to provide for their children (2013).

Individuals react to stress differently depending on the connection of the event to the person's values and goals (Park, 1997).

Student-parents have different values and goals than traditional students because they have to provide for their children (Brown, 2007).

Still, stress is not always viewed as unfavorable because stressful situations could lead to personal growth (Park, 1997).

Therefore, although student-parents experienced pressure as a result of multiple responsibilities, they still performed academically well. However, when a lack of social integration caused stress, student-parents were less likely to remain in school because they felt they did not belong there (Jiménez, 2017).

Although student-parents can achieve high academic performance despite the high levels of stress that accompanied their multiple responsibilities, they still need a social support system to feel motivated to continue their studies. There are valid scholarly reasons why student parents do not succeed in higher Education, such as a lack of social integration, welfare requirements, and stress on their children (Fenster, 2004).

When the social categories that student-parents identify with are combined together, challenges can be seen as more prominent for some parents than others. Because factors such as racial discrepancies are not noted, academic attainment alone is not a good indicator of understanding the experience of marginalized student-parents. Further research is needed to discover better ways to support student-parents.

Exploring the intersectional challenges that they face because of their multiple identities will provide an understanding of the privileges and barriers they experience and help us move towards embedding reliable support systems in educational institutions. Additionally, to provide a deeper understanding of which solutions work for some student-parents and which work for others, studies on student-parents should target participants from different schools and different socioeconomic backgrounds.

Education and Student-Parents

Research demonstrates that working concurrently with school significantly decreases the odds of completing a bachelor's degree on time (Zarifa et al., 2018).

Additionally, the multiple obligations that student parents juggle with children, work, and being more likely to commute from off-campus make student parents more likely to have "stop and start" college trajectories (Zarifa et al., 2018). As discussed above, the financial constraints that student parents face decrease the likelihood of remaining in school and graduating within six years. It is not surprising, then, that past research suggests that increasing financial aid to students decreases the amount of time it takes to graduate (Zarifa et al., 2018).

Retention Fifty-two percent of undergraduate student parents drop out of college within six years of enrolling, compared with 32% of non-parents (GAO, 2019).

A driving factor in this disparity in retention is the "time poverty" – the lack of time student parents have for rest and leisure after taking into account the time spent on work, school, home, and parenting duties – that student parents experience, making continuing school untenable for many (Ascend at the Aspen Institute , 2019).

GPA Student parents may be less likely to graduate on time or remain enrolled in classes, yet past research suggests that undergraduate student parents have higher GPAs compared to non-parent students (Reichlin Cruse, Holtzman, et al., 2019). One-third of undergraduate student parents have a GPA of 3.5 or higher (Reichlin Cruse, Holtzman, et al., 2019).

Success among Student-Parents

Previous research suggests that despite the challenges student parents face, as a group, they are extremely motivated to succeed academically (Goodman & Reddy, 2019). Student parents, particularly single mothers, are motivated by the well-documented positive intergenerational benefits – short-term and long-term – that their pursuit of higher education will have on their children (Goodman & Reddy, 2019). Single mothers in Minnesota who graduate with a bachelor's degree are 75% less likely to live in poverty than single mothers whose highest level of Education is high school (Reichlin Cruse, Milli et al., 2019).

The positive impact of a mother's Education on children includes intergenerational benefits beyond increased financial stability for households (Reichlin Cruse, Milli et al., 2019).

Educated mothers are more likely to create high-quality home learning environments for children and utilize parenting strategies that incorporate learning, as well as serve as role models for higher education achievement (Magnuson, 2007; Monoghan, 2016).

Children of educated mothers have improved cognitive development, higher test scores, and better academic outcomes compared to children of mothers with high school degrees or less (Magnuson, 2007).

Mothers with college degrees are also more likely to invest in child health-promoting behaviors, which may be why children of more educated mothers have improved health outcomes (Prickett & Augustine, 2016).

As adults, children with educated mothers are more likely to graduate from high school, attend college, and graduate from college themselves (Monoghan, 2016). This leads to increased wages and creates an intergenerational cycle of family economic security (Reichlin Cruse, Holtzman, et al., 2019; Reichlin Cruse, Milli et al., 2019).

Assistance from Institutions

These professors allowed deadlines to be adapted and course evaluations to be rescheduled in cases of emergencies, and they worked to support their students as persons (Branscomb, 2006; Medved & Heisler, 2002; Robertson et al., 2012).

Student-parents denote higher levels of satisfaction when working with such professors. Student-parents frequently request or note appreciation for more accessible class times. Due to the rigid structuring of courses at many universities, student-parents must decide whether they will place their role as a student before their role as a parent or vice versa.

Some individuals do not have a choice and must limit the number of courses they take at a time in order to care for their child (van Rhijn, 2014), which may negatively impact the student financially by lengthening the course of Education.

Additionally, most students request the ability to be home with their family in the evening and are again limited by avoiding night courses or exams. Students place high value on the ability to establish an evening routine with their families (Robertson et al., 2012; van Rhijn, 2014).

Research shows that several support services available through the university decrease the levels of stress student-parents feel in various aspects of life. Accessible, affordable, and flexible childcare tops the list of desired services (Bussey, 2002; Cerven, 2013; Lovell, 2014; Moreau & Kerner, 2012; Robertson et al., 2012).

While most parents feel capable of locating childcare during the day, they see a need for childcare that offers evening care or drop-in hours at an affordable rate. Student-parents raising children on their own request these flexible services at higher rates than married or cohabitating parents (Robertson et al., 2012). Students with children recognize the need for more affordable housing located on or near campus.

Many graduate students note this as an area requiring improvement, despite having an easier time accessing affordable family housing when compared to undergraduate students raising a child on their own. These younger students are less likely to enter school with a stable full- or part-time job or a partner who works full-time (Robertson et al., 2012).

Not surprisingly, many undergraduate students with children struggle with financial stability. Quality of living decreases as finances decrease, meaning many student-parents must decide how to prioritize their money when caring for a family, financing their Education, and meeting other demands of life (Robertson et al., 2012).

Beyond the tangible support services institutions can offer to student-parents, many students desire opportunities for connection. Students with children possess the same desire to interact with their peers outside of the classroom, both with and without 15 their children. Students feel excluded due to the majority of campus programs being scheduled in the evening (van Rhijn, 2014).

Additionally, student-parents desire increased opportunities to connect with other student-parents on campus. These individuals "reported feeling isolated and socially excluded" as well as desiring relationships with others who understand their life situation (van Rhijn, 2014, p. 5).

Connections with peers may be able to offer some comfort for students with children as they balance various roles in life. This role conflict has also been shown to decrease when opportunities for counseling are available (Cerven, 2013). By creating more opportunities for student-parents to process their experiences, these individuals may feel better understood and supported by campus staff who not only listen to their needs but help them find solutions.

Counselors should be trained to understand the specific needs of the student-parent population in order to make these services most effective (Cerven, 2013; van Rhijn, 2014).

In conclusion, studies reveal the common needs of all students with children that could be better served by institutions of higher education.

The literature significantly notes that, when not supported by the institution, the undergraduate student-parent population faces the greatest risk of dropout (Lovell, 2014).

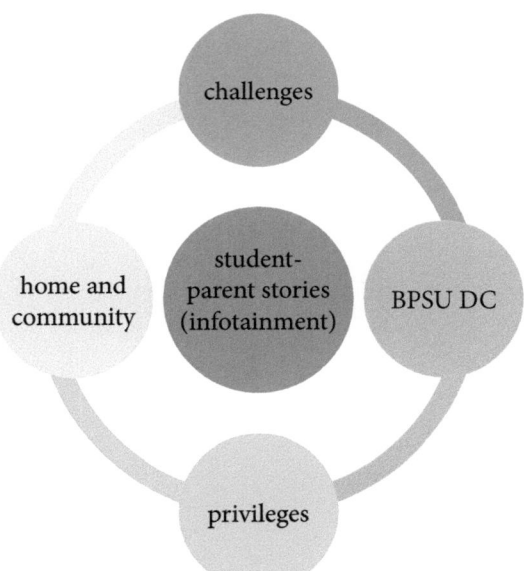

This includes the continuous direction where the four small plates represent the places and the sources of the stories among the student-parent. This also includes infotainment, which is the main output of the study.

"IT'S NOT WHAT YOU LOOK AT THAT MATTERS. IT'S WHAT YOU SEE."

Henry David Thoreau, essayist, and poet

Part I: Lived Experiences of the student-parents through their challenges and Privileges

Self-Reliance is a Must

The participants agreed that in times of need, one of their challenges is self-reliance. Most of them, the time when they have to fetch their children while having their classes at BPSU-DC, they have to make the decision for themselves for them to pick up their children on their own; they are not asking anything from their parents or even significant ones. Most of them, because they are single parents, have to endure the pain of being alone in terms of decision-making. This made them feel weak and always feel the self-pity. They always see themselves as different from other people since they are doing parental tasks, and this is not an easy job since the children that they have are all dependent. It is always hard also to think, according to them, to multi-tasking, some are doing their job outside the institution, and some are breadwinners. It was not easy, and all they have to do is to rely on themselves. Additionally, student-parents desire increased opportunities to connect with other student-parents on campus. These individuals "reported feeling isolated and socially excluded" as well as desiring relationships with others who understand their life situation (van Rhijn, 2014, p. 5). Connections with peers may be able to offer some comfort for students with children as they balance various roles in life. This role conflict has also been shown to decrease when opportunities for counseling are available (Cerven, 2013). By creating more opportunities for student-parents to process their experiences, these individuals may feel better understood and supported by campus staff who not only listen to their needs but help them find solutions. Some of the answers from the responses are as follows:

> P5: "I have experienced many challenges; one of the challenges is that I cannot cope

with our lessons because I am taking care of my child and ended up missing school work. I felt so frustrated at that time, and I don't want to study anymore."

P3: "As a student parent, I have experienced a lot of challenges. One of those challenges is that I experienced life without anyone's help because of the pandemic. It is hard for me to study while taking care of my son and do the household chores yung oras ko sa pag aaral mas kumokonti dahil sa sabay sabay na gawain and at the same time pag aalaga sa anak ko. I am also scared because if ever na may pumasok na stranger sa bahay which is bahay ng in-laws ko dahil nga naabutan sila ng lockdown sa amin karinderya, no one will help me dahil hindi rin stable ang internet connection namin that time. Di ako makapag focus noon sa pag aaral pero inaalagaan ko mabuti yung anak ko."

They also revealed that since they rely on themselves, they mostly get real-time for themselves. They forget that there is a ME time, and they need also this to start an additional journey with less stress. They believe that they can do it, but overall they are consumed with their time, and this makes them vulnerable to anxiety, self-harm, and such. But overall, the participants were strong, and they had chosen to fight the battle. Just fight and go over with their lives strong and powerful, with a growth mindset.

> P1: "Nawawalan ng oras para sa sarili. Naubos na lahat ng energy it can lessen the time for a review since a child needs a lot of attention. na pressure dahil maraming nagtitiwala na makapagtapos ako at sa sabay sabay na paper works"

Some, because they are studying, have to rely on themselves to review and focus while doing all these circuses in their lives. No one can do that for them except them, no one can take the exam for them or make the assignments for them or answer the oral recitation for them, so they are the most powerful weapon that they can have, and this makes them feel a roller coaster emotions thinking that these are challenges and barriers.

> P2: "My barriers in studying are that I can't focus on my studying and end up with low scores or grades in our subjects, and one of the barriers also is the lack of time management because I don't know what I

will do first If I will take care of my baby or do my missing tasks. But gratefully, I made it; I have overcome that kind of situation."

This participant agreed that missing out on some school activities has taken a toll on their school grades since they have to set a list of priorities.

P3: "Ito yung may mga oras o pagkakataon na hindi ka makakapag participate sa mga bagay bagay like school activities for some reasons tulad na lang na emergency sa bagay or kailangan ka ng anak mo. Like what I've said dumadami na ang responsibilities mo dahil hindi nalang sarili mo ang iintindihin mo."

Bounded by Time, by Responsibilities

They agreed that being in the situation of a parent means more than just being a parent, especially during the pandemic. They were tested, and their faith in God has also been tested. They thought of many avenues to identify and to make to fulfill their dreams and continue with financial sustenance for their young ones and their children, but most of them could not easily get jobs since they were still studying. They are mostly bounded by time as a student, and this makes it more challenging for them. Although many community college campuses have student-parent support programs, some student participation requirements create barriers that ultimately prevent them from graduating (Austin, 2013). Findings suggest that the primary reason low-income parents do not continue their higher education is due to the criteria instituted in federally-funded welfare programs. The required time commitment negatively impacts academic performance and thus acts as a barrier for parents; parents must comply with the programs' requirements to receive and perpetuate their financial aid, yet the requirements become a significant obstacle to achieving those very academic outcomes meant to help them support their families (Austin, 2003, p.100). Working to fulfill welfare requirements while attending college also creates collateral damage to the family unit. The long hours required to participate in both work and school and the stress involved in juggling such responsibilities can contribute to the neglect of young children. Furthermore, wages from this work combined with financial aid may not even be enough to cover living expenses for single parents and their children. Due to the fear of housing insecurity, many of these students withdraw from college altogether in order to work full-time and be able to Brenda Coronel afford a better living situation. With all of these factors, work and enrollment requirements for federal assistance allow student parents neither academic nor financial stability.

Another thing that makes their job not easy peasy has tasks that are special, just like being in a world of autism, where the child is autistic and has special needs while the mother of the participant is 63 years old. Life here could get touch each and everybody's hearts. Where one might ask, what are these challenges, and how come these challenges are a burden alone for the participants?

> P4: *"I am also a single parent, the barrier to my studying is no one to take care of my son when I am at school; it is hard for me to leave him with my mom because my mom is 63 years old. She is old for taking care of a 2 years old toddler diagnosed with Autism."*

Their time is broken down into many parts of themselves. Sometimes, when they are in the pit of their anxiety and sadness, they are thinking of just giving up, but their children are those that give them motivation and will to carry on. This is true with the statements of the participants:

P5: *"The challenges that I've experienced as a student parent are the responsibilities of being a parent at home and a student at a school. Time management, it is so hard to balance parental duties and academic activities. I don't have enough time to study, I always attend class late, and spending quality time with my son is so hard to do because of having a lot of academic requirements."*

It was seen based on the answer of the participant that having more responsibilities includes the consumption of time. Since everybody is bounded by time, they are also bounded with so much responsibilities. Their responsibilities and the willingness to become part of these equal responsibilities make them hard to appreciate the remaining time that they have for everything that they might be doing. Their responsibilities in school, at the house, and even in their job make it more painful and complicated. Likewise, they believed that whenever the school is giving lots of lessons, or even during their on-the-job training, their tasks are increasing and getting more and more tasks to accomplish.

There were so many things that needed the participant's attention, care, and indeed strength, just like taking care of their children always and especially during health problems which may consume too much time:

> P2: *"Pag aalaga sa anak sa gabi kaya napupuyat pa rin palagi. Malayo sa mga printing shop at nasasabay sa pag aalaga kaya di nakakagawa minsan sa oras yung mga activity. Kailangan umuwi ng maaga dahil may anak na inaalagaan kaya kap may groupings sa school tapos may meeting hindi ako makasama. Always late din ako dahil kapag nagising anak ko minsan papatulugin ko pa ulit para makapasok ako."*

The researcher is not new to this type of situation since the researcher herself is a student-parent and is very much sure that being a student-parent is not an easy task. It is easy to just cut all the connections and just stay away from the responsibilities, but since Education has given people the ability to change and the ability to go through life with changing perspectives, the participants, together with the researcher, are surviving and getting all themselves, their pieces together to become whole and strong.

The Beam of Balance: Tool for Success

P1: "Ang hirap ibalance yung oras lalo na pag nagkasabay sabay as a student teacher and as a parent ng 2 bata napakaraming nakaabang na trabaho sa school paper works pag uwi sa bahay mag aasikaso ng mga anak ko pag nakatulog na yung mga bata gawa ulit ng mga kailangan tapusin para sa school halos wala ng tulog walang pahinga pero kinakaya yun ang no mas mahirap na sitwasyon kung may sakit yung anak ko tapos sumabay pa mga need ipasa sa school sobrang hirap pero kinakaya naman ngayon paba ako susuko almost 4 years na akong nag aaral ng may mga anak ngayon pa ba kung kailan malapit nako sa finish line."

Whenever they juggle with one or two tasks at the same time, the participants revealed that they are feeling obnoxious. Their feelings of happiness are all removed, and they think of getting more and more assistance from other people, but balancing the beam, as they say, requires perseverance and toughness, not just physically but also especially emotional strength. While some might give up, the participants always look at how they had been balancing their lives, although this time, and this made them stronger and more powerful, their mindset is a giveaway strength for them. They think that there are other people who are feeling the same way, and they are happy about it. They love being a parent. Yes, it is a challenge, full of sacrifices, but in the end, success is what it may bring.

> P3: "Ang pagiging estudyante at isang ina ay dalawang bagay na pareho ng komplikado. Bilang isang student parent maraming challenges ang dapat na kaharapin. Kabilang na dito ang nagiging komplikado ng schedule. Dapat marunong kang mag measure ng mga gagawin mo. Alam mo dapat ang oras na para sa school works at oras para sa anak mo na kadalasan at nagsasabay pa. Pangalawa financial bilang estudyante ang hirap mag budget para sa mga dapat mo dalhin nandyan ang para sa baon school requirements at iba pa, what more kung nanay kapa gatas diaper at iba pang needs ng bata. Next is when it comes to emotions kung ano naba lagay mo mentally stress sa school works at sa pag aalaga lalo na kung mag isa mo lang itinataguyod pareho dadaan ka talaga sa stress at pag nagkataon mapupunta pa sa

depression. Kaya mahalaga talaga na may support ka from others. Lastly physically isa sa puhunan ng estudyante at isang ina ang pagiging malusog. Pero paano kung puyat kana sa pag aalaga puyat kapa at pagod sa school activities. Hindi madali maging isang ina lalo na kung isa ka ring estudyante."

In terms of the privileges, there are highlighted themes which were reflected below:

So that Others May Learn from It

"Others might learn from our story," as one of the participants stated. Their stories, including the story of the researcher herself, are a success story that others may wonder and marvel at. Previous research suggests that despite the challenges student parents face, as a group, they are extremely motivated to succeed academically (Goodman & Reddy, 2019). Student parents, particularly single mothers, are motivated by the well-documented positive intergenerational benefits – short-term and long-term – that their pursuit of higher education will have on their children (Goodman & Reddy, 2019). Single mothers in Minnesota who graduate with a

bachelor's degree are 75% less likely to live in poverty than single mothers whose highest level of Education is high school (Reichlin Cruse, Milli et al., 2019). The positive impact of a mother's Education on children includes intergenerational benefits beyond increased financial stability for households (Reichlin Cruse, Milli et al., 2019). Educated mothers are more likely to create high-quality home learning environments for children and utilize parenting strategies that incorporate learning, as well as serve as role models for higher education achievement (Magnuson, 2007; Monoghan, 2016). Children of educated mothers have improved cognitive development, higher test scores, and better academic outcomes compared to children of mothers with high school degrees or less (Magnuson, 2007). Mothers with college degrees are also more likely to invest in child health-promoting behaviors, which may be why children of more educated mothers have improved health outcomes (Prickett & Augustine, 2016). As adults, children with educated mothers are more likely to graduate from high school, attend college, and graduate from college themselves (Monoghan, 2016). This leads to increased wages and creates an intergenerational cycle of family economic security (Reichlin Cruse, Holtzman, et al., 2019; Reichlin Cruse, Milli et al., 2019).

Others might see and feel that in everything that participants do, being a strong individual has its consequences, and being positive requires more than just accepting one's own faith. It is a strong individual who accepts their fate in life and does positive things about it that is a great privilege that others may learn from it.

> P2: *"The privilege I have experienced in school is that my situation is understandable by other teachers so that they are being considerate in terms of giving grades. They try to support me where I am and help me get to where I want to be. Also, it is a privilege when someone listens to my story when nobody wants to in our home."*

Education begets Education

Since the BPSU DC caters the Education, its core values and mission through education offers varieties of comprehension for the situation they had with them. They believed that Education begets Education since their teachers are very considerate and give them all the understanding they can get. They are also privileged to become part of the institution, and it's also exciting for them to think that they will soon have their own terms, which they will become teachers of their own and they will have their own tasks and may forward the blessings which they can give to others in times of needs through Education. These professors allowed deadlines to be adapted and course evaluations to be rescheduled in cases of emergencies, and they worked to support their students as persons (Branscomb, 2006; Medved & Heisler, 2002; Robertson et al., 2012). Student-parents denote higher levels of satisfaction when working with such professors. Student-parents frequently request or note appreciation for more accessible class times. Due to the rigid structuring of courses at many universities, student-parents must decide whether they will place their role as a student before their role as a parent or vice versa. Some individuals do not have a choice and must limit the number of courses they take at a time in order to care for their child (van Rhijn, 2014), which may negatively impact the student financially by lengthening the course of Education. Additionally, most students request the ability to be home with their family in the evening and are again limited by avoiding night courses or exams. Students place high value on the ability to establish an evening routine with their families (Robertson et al., 2012; van Rhijn, 2014).

P1: *"The professor and instructor in BPSU are very understanding in terms of being late, late submission of the other activities, and sometimes if I suddenly did not attend class. Most of all, they allow me to attend class with my son even though sometimes my son interrupts our class discussion."*

P2: *"Bilang student teacher napakasarap lang maranasan na nirerespeto ako at tinawag na Ma'am ng mga student's at syempre napaka swerte ko dahil as a parent ok lang na isama ko paminsan yung anak ko sa school lalo na kung walang magbabantay.napakalaking karangalan din na nirerespeto ako ng mga kapwa ko mag aaral na hindi iba ang turing sa akin kahit na ako ay may anak na at lalo na sa mahal kung BPSU na tumatanggap ng mga student's kahit na may mga anak pa ito dahil hindi naman humihinto ang pangarap kung naging maaga man tayong naging magulang nagkaanak lang tayo pero hindi tayo nawalan ng karapatan para mangarap at mag aral."*

Opportunities to Graduate and Become Professional

They are given the set of skills in the institution amidst what they have, and even though their challenges, problems, and issues are skyscraping, the institution is there; they are determined to assist the student-parents. This makes them more positive and more determined to fight the challenges in life, and they consider being in the BPSU DC a privilege, always a privilege.

> P4: *"The privileges that I have experienced in school is I have a lot of opportunities to grab; one of the opportunities is that the school I am entering is a free tuition school. I believe being a student parent is not the end, but it is the start or beginning. I've learned that I have many goals that I need to achieve; I need to focus on my studies so that I will have a brighter future someday."*

> P2: *"Ang pagtanggap nila sa isang tulad namin. Ang pag allow na mag aral at patuloy na mangarap kahit na may anak na. Kasama na rin dito ang consideration na natatanggap natin from teachers and classmates kung minsan nagkakaroon ng*

delay sa pagpapasa ng mga requirements at kung minsan di pag participate sa mga school activities. At pinakamahalaga sa lahat emotional support galing sa mga taong totoong may malasakit at nakakaintindi sayo."

Evidence shows that investment in supportive services for student parents leads to a strong return on investment. Improving undergraduate student parents' outcomes is a critical component in college and universities' efforts to promote equity in education access and outcomes (Reichlin Cruse, Holtzman, et al., 2019). In order to improve outcomes (such as graduation, retention, and GPA) for this diverse group of traditionally underrepresented students, higher education institutions need to understand what evidence-based practices exist to address their needs as parents (Pendelton and Atella, 2020). Research shows that several support services available through the university decrease the levels of stress student-parents feel in various aspects of life. Accessible, affordable, and flexible childcare tops the list of desired services (Bussey, 2002; Cerven, 2013; Lovell, 2014; Moreau & Kerner, 2012; Robertson et al., 2012). While most parents feel capable of locating childcare during the day, they see a need for childcare that offers evening care or drop-in hours at an affordable rate. Student-parents raising children on their own request these flexible services at higher rates than married or cohabitating parents (Robertson et al., 2012). Students with children recognize the need for more affordable housing located on or near campus. Not surprisingly, many undergraduate students with children struggle with financial stability. Quality of living decreases as finances decrease, meaning many student-parents must decide how to prioritize their money when caring for a family, financing their Education, and meeting other demands of life (Robertson et al., 2012). Beyond the tangible support services institutions can offer to student-parents, many students desire opportunities for connection. Students with children possess the same desire to interact with their peers outside of the classroom, both with and without their children. Students feel excluded due to the majority of campus programs being scheduled in the evening (van Rhijn, 2014). Counselors should be trained to understand the specific needs of the student-parent population in order to make these services most effective (Cerven, 2013; van Rhijn, 2014). In conclusion, studies reveal the common needs of all students with children that could be better served by institutions of higher education. The literature significantly notes that, when not supported by the institution, the undergraduate student-parent population faces the greatest risk of dropout (Lovell, 2014).

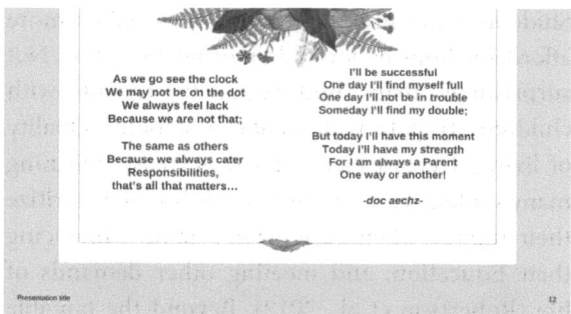

"*LET US REMEMBER: ONE BOOK, ONE PEN, ONE CHILD, AND ONE TEACHER CAN CHANGE THE WORLD.*"

Malala Yousafzai, Pakistani activist for Education

Part I: Lived Experiences of the student-parents through their challenges and Privileges

Self-Reliance is a Must

The participants agreed that in times of need, one of their challenges is self-reliance. Most of them, during the times when they have to fetch their children while having their classes at BPSU-DC, have to make the decision for themselves for them to pick up their children on their own; they are not asking anything from their parents or even significant ones. Most of them, because they are single parents, have to endure the pain of being alone in terms of decision-making. This made them feel weak and always feel the self-pity. They always see themselves as different from other people since they are doing parental tasks, and this is not an easy job since the children that they have are all dependent. It is always hard also to think, according to them, to multi-tasking, some are doing their job outside the institution, and some are breadwinners. It was not easy, and all they have to do is to rely on themselves.

Bounded by Time, by Responsibilities

They agreed that being in the situation of a parent means more than just being a parent, especially during the pandemic. They were tested, and their faith in God has also been tested. They thought of many avenues to identify and to make to fulfill their dreams and continue with financial sustenance for their young ones and their children, but most of them could not easily get jobs since they were still studying. They are mostly bounded by time as a student, and this makes it more challenging for them. Another thing that makes their job not easy peasy has tasks that are special, just like being in a world of autism, where the child is autistic and has special needs while the mother of the participant is 63 years old.

The Beam of Balance: Tool for Success

Whenever they juggle with one or two tasks at the same time, the participants revealed that they are feeling obnoxious. Their feelings of happiness are all removed, and they think of getting more and more assistance from other people, but balancing the beam, as they say, requires perseverance and toughness, not just physically but also especially emotional strength. While some might give up, the participants always look at how they had been balancing their lives, although this time, and this made them stronger and more powerful, their mindset is a giveaway strength for them. They think that there are other people who are feeling the same way, and they are happy about it. They love being a parent. Yes, it is a challenge, full of sacrifices, but in the end, success is what it may bring.

In terms of the privileges, there are highlighted themes which were reflected below:

So that Others May Learn from It

"Others might learn from our story," as one of the participants stated. Their stories, including the story of the researcher herself, are a success story that others may wonder and marvel at. Others might see and feel that in everything that we do, being a strong individual has its consequences, and being positive requires more than just accepting one's own faith it is being a strong individual who accepts their fate in life and doing positive things about it, that is a great privilege that others may learn from it.

Education begets Education

Since the BPSU DC caters the Education, its core values and mission through education offers varieties of comprehension for the situation they had with them. They believed that Education begets Education since their teachers are very considerate and give them all the understanding they can get. They are also privileged to become part of the institution, and it's also exciting for them to think that they will soon have their own terms, which they will become teachers of their own and they will have their own tasks and may forward the blessings which they can give to others in times of needs through Education.

Opportunities to Graduate and Become Professional

They are given the set of skills in the institution amidst what they have, and even though their challenges, problems, and issues are skyscraping, the institution is there; they are determined to assist the student-parents. This makes them more positive and more determined to fight the challenges in life, and they consider being in the BPSU DC a privilege, always a privilege.

Conclusions

In terms of the Lived Experiences of the student-parents through their challenges and Privileges, the themes presented are *Self-Reliance is a Must*; *Bounded by Time, by Responsibilities*; *The Beam of Balance: Tool for Success.*

In terms of the privileges, there are highlighted themes which were: *So that Others May Learn from It*; *Education begets Education*; *Opportunities to Graduate and Become Professional.*

In terms of the Infographic Material gathered from the Data, this represents heartfelt stories of the experiences of the student-parent through their challenges and privileges.

Recommendations

1. A new set of participants might be included in the student-parent studies to explore more variations and responses.

2. Using an ethnographic approach, the qualitative design might be included in the study for more highlights and a deeper connection of the data.
3. Use the infotainment/infographic tool to deliver awareness and make this another set of studies for orientation/information dissemination.

REFERENCES

Quotes. (2023). https://scots.college/ten-inspirational-quotes-to-encourage-parents/

Universal Class Positive Parenting. (2023). https://www.universalclass.com/articles/self-help/various-theories-and-aspects-of-positive-parenting.htm#:~:text=These%20are%20positive%20psychology%2C%20parenting,learning%20theory%2C%20and%20child%20development.&text=Positive%20parenting%20is%20focused%20on,of%20optimal%20growth%20and%20development.

Court, P. (2018). Supporting Student-P ting Student-Parents: A Qualitativ ents: A Qualitative Explor e Exploration of the ation of the Online Presence of Support at Postsecondary Institutions. *Pillars at Taylor University.* https://pillars.taylor.edu/cgi/viewcontent.cgi?article=1118&context=mahe.

Abrams, H. G., & Jernigan, L. P. (1984). Academic support services and the success of high-risk college students. American Educational Research Journal, 21, 261–274. doi:10.3102/00028312021002261

Astin, A. W. (1984). Student involvement: A developmental theory for higher Education. Journal of College Student Personnel, 25(4), 297–308.

Bettinger, E. P., Boatman, A., & Long, B. T. (2013). Student supports Developmental Education and other academic programs. Future of Children, 23(1), 93–115. doi:10.1353/foc.2013.0003

Bowen, G. A. (2009). Document analysis as a qualitative research method. Qualitative Research Journal, 9(2), 27–40. doi:10.3316/QRJ0902027

Branscomb, K. A. (2006). Undergraduate students as parents: Managing multiple roles during emerging adulthood (Doctoral dissertation). Retrieved from IDEALS database. (Order No. 3242799)

Brooks, R. (2015). Social and spatial disparities in emotional responses to Education: Feelings of "guilt" among student-parents. British Educational Research Journal, 41, 505–519. doi:10.1002/berj.3154

Bussey, J. C. (2002). Babes in the classroom: Reflections on accommodation. Reflections: Narratives of Professional Helping, 8(2), 29–41. Retrieved from 32 https://reflectionsnarrativesofprofessionalhelping.org/index.php/Reflections/article/view/894/716

Cerven, C. (2013). Public and private lives: Institutional structures and personal supports in low-income single mothers' educational pursuits. Education Policy Analysis Archives, 21(17). Retrieved from http://epaa.asu.edu/ojs/

Çivitci, A. (2015). The moderating role of positive and negative affect on the relationship between perceived social support and stress in college students. Educational Sciences: Theory and Practice, 15, 565–573. doi:10.12738/estp.2015.3.2553

Creswell, J. W. (2013). Qualitative inquiry & research design: Choosing among five approaches (3rd ed.). Los Angeles, CA: Sage Publications.

Darling, R. A. (2015). Creating an institutional academic advising culture that supports commuter student success. New Directions for Student Services, 2015(150), 87– 96. doi:10.1002/ss.20130

de Oliveira Urpia, A. M., & da Rocha Sampaio, S. M. (2012). Being a mother and an undergraduate student: The dialogical process of becoming a mother in the academic context. In J. Valsiner, K. Uriko, & A. C. de Sousa Bastos (Eds.), Cultural dynamics of women's lives (pp. 467–487). Charlotte, NC: Information Age Publishing.

Erikson, E. (1994). Identity: Youth and crisis. New York, NY: W. W. Norton & Company. Field, K. (2017, April 16). College, with kids. The Chronicle of Higher Education. Retrieved from http://www.chronicle.com/article/College-With-Kids/239793?cid=at&utm_source=at&utm_medium=en&elqTrackId=40518b55333 31440f5a2d24f38ad2cf8db&elq=6ffe7eff15b-f4caa90fc042f17fd0f92&elqaid=135 27&elqa-t=1&elqCampaignId=5618

Flores, A. (2014). How public universities can promote access and success for all students. Retrieved from Center for American Progress website: https://cdn.americanprogress.org/wp-content/uploads/2014/09/FloresCase-Studybrief.pdf

Gault, B., Reichlin, L., & Roman. (2014). College affordability for low-income adults: Improving returns on investment for families and society. Retrieved from Institute for Women's Policy Research website: https://iwpr.org/wpcontent/uploads/wpallimport/files/iwpr-export/publications/C412-college%20affordability.pdf

Gonchar, N. (1995). College-student mothers and on-site child care: Luxury or necessity? Social Work in Education, 17, 226–234. doi:10.1093/cs/17.4.226

Harmon, M. (2013). The impact of institutional support services, policies, and programs on the completion and graduation of African American students enrolled at select two-year colleges in Ohio (Doctoral dissertation). Retrieved from University of Toledo Digital Repository. (Order No. 94)

Indiana University School of Education. (2017). Listings. Retrieved from http://carnegieclassifications.iu.edu/lookup/standard.php#standard_basic2005_list

Kloss, R. J. (1994). A nudge is best: Helping students through the Perry Scheme of intellectual development. College Teaching, 42, 151–158. doi:10.1080/87567555.1994.9926847 34

Lovell, E. D. (2014). College students who are parents need equitable services for retention. Journal of College Student Retention: Research, Theory and Practice, 16, 187–202. doi:10.2190/CS.16.2.b

Luyckx, K., Goossens, L., & Soenens, B. (2006). A developmental contextual perspective on identity construction in emerging adulthood: Change dynamics in commitment formation and commitment evaluation. Developmental Psychology, 42, 366–380. doi:10.1037/0012-1649.42.2.366

Markle, G. (2015). Factors influencing persistence among nontraditional university students. Adult Education Quarterly, 65, 267–285. doi:10.1177/0741713615583085

Medved, C. E., & Heisler, J. (2002). A negotiated order exploration of critical student-faculty interactions: Student-parents manage multiple roles. Communication Education, 51(2), 105–120. doi:10.1080/03634520216510

Moreau, M.-P., & Kerner, C. (2012). Supporting student parents in higher Education: A policy analysis. Retrieved from the Nuffield Foundation website: https://www.nuffieldfoundation.org/sites/default/files/files/Moreau%20Student%2 0Parent%20report%20-%20Full%20report%20October%202012.pdf

Munday, L. A. (1976). College access for nontraditional students. The Journal of Higher Education, 47(6), 681. doi:10.2307/1979122

National Center for Education Statistics. (2016). Digest of Education Statistics, 2015. Retrieved from https://nces.ed.gov/programs/digest/d15/tables/dt15_303.40.asp?current=yes 35

Ritchie, R. A., Meca, A., Madrazo, V. L., Schwartz, S. J., Hardy, S. A., Zamboanga, B. L., … Lee, R. M. (2013). Identity dimensions and related processes in emerging adulthood: Helpful or harmful? Journal of Clinical Psychology, 69, 415–432. doi:10.1002/jclp.21960

Robertson, A. S., Weider, A., Weider, J., & Morey, P. (2012). When the nontraditional becomes traditional: Addressing the needs of student-parents in Higher Education (I-Parent Report). University of Illinois Urbana-Champaign. Retrieved from https://www.ideals.illinois.edu/handle/2142/50057

Taniguchi, H., & Kaufman, G. (2005). Degree completion among nontraditional college students. Social Science Quarterly, 86, 912–927. doi:10.1111/j.0038- 4941.2005.00363.x

van Rhijn, T. M. (2014). Barriers, enablers, and strategies for success identified by undergraduate student parents. CJNSE/RCJCÉ, 5(1). Retrieved from http://cjnse.journalhosting.ucalgary.ca/ojs2/index.php/cjnse/article/view/207

Acevedo-Gil, N., Santos, R. E., Alonso, L., & Solorzano, D. G. (2015). Latinas/os in community college developmental education: Increasing moments of academic and interpersonal validation. Journal of Hispanic Higher Education, 14(2), 101-127. https://doi.org/10.1177/1538192715572893

Austin, S. A., & McDermott, K. A. (2003). College persistence among single mothers after welfare reform: An exploratory study. Journal of College Student Retention: Research, Theory & Practice, 5(2), 93-113. https://doi.org/10.2190/UQLXBQX6-BYW0-YT89

Bowleg, L. (2012). The problem with the phrase women and minorities: intersectionality—an important theoretical framework for public health. American Journal of public health, 102(7), 1267-1273. https://doi.org/10.2105/AJPH.2012.300750

Brown, R. L. (2007). College Females as Mothers: Balancing the Roles of Student and Motherhood. ABNF Journal, 18(1), 25. Retrieved from https://pubmed. ncbi.nlm.nih.gov/18402354/

Brown, V., Nichols, T. R. (2013). Pregnant and parenting students on campus: Policy and program implications for a growing population. Educational Policy, 27(3), 499-530. https://doi. org/10.1177/0895904812453995

Cho, S., Crenshaw, K. W., & McCall, L. (2013). Toward a field of intersectionality studies: Theory, applications, and praxis. Signs: Journal of Women in Culture and Society, 38(4), 785- 810. https://www.jstor.org/stable/10.1086/669608

CollegeSimply. (2019). Rio Hondo College Student Demographics. Retrieved from https://www.

collegesimply.com/colleges/california/rio-hondo-college/students/.

Fenster, J. (2004). Can welfare mothers hack it in college? A comparison of achievement between TANF recipients and general population community college students. Journal of College Student Retention: Research, Theory & Practice, 5(4) 421-430. https://doi.org/10.2190/1077-JQAR-PL1G-HMEB

Anderson & Clark, J & J, (2016) Institute for Women's Policy Research the analysis of American Community Survey Brenda Coronel 65 Microdata Integrated Public Use Microdata Series, Version 6.0. Retrieved from https://iwpr.org/publications/status-ofwomen-fact-sheet-2018/

Jiménez, H., & Oliva, N. (2017). Latina Student Mothers' Trenzas de Identidades in the Community College. Association of Mexican American Educators Journal, 11(2), 111-132. https://doi.org/10.24974/amae.11.2.352

Ling, T. S. (2002). Lifting voices: Towards Equal Education for pregnant and parenting students in new york city. Fordham Urban Law Journal, 29(6),2387-2412.   https://ir.lawnet.fordham.edu/ulj/vol29/iss6/4/

Merriam, S. B. (2002). Introduction to qualitative research. Qualitative research in practice: Examples for discussion and analysis, 1(1), 1-17.

Park, C. L., & Folkman, S. (1997). Meaning in the Context of Stress and Coping. Review of General Psychology, 1(2), 115– 144. https://doi.org/10.1037/1089-2680.1.2.115

Pérez Huber, L., Malagón, M. C., Ramirez, B. R., Gonzalez, L. C., Jimenez, A., & Vélez, V. N. (2015). Still Falling through the Cracks: Revisiting the Latina/o Education Pipeline. CSRC Research Report. Number 19. UCLA Chicano Studies Research Center. https://files.eric.ed.gov/fulltext/ED574691.pdf

Steele, C. M. (1997). A threat in the air: How stereotypes shape intellectual identity and performance. American Psychologist, 52(6), 613–629.   https://doi.org/10.1037/0003-066X.52.6.613

Coronel,B. (2023). *The Lived Experience of Community College Student-Parents.* https://escholarship.org/content/qt4dp449pz/qt-4dp449pz_noSplash_13f67267902fa4f-0c3967f3ef5ce1023.pdf?t=qdzeun.

Ascend at the Aspen Institute. (2019). Accelerating postsecondary success for parents identifying

and addressing mental health needs. (2019).
https://ascend.aspeninstitute.org/resources/
accelerating-postsecondary-successfor-
parents-identifying-and-addressing-mental-
health-needs/

Goodman, S., & Reddy, M. (2019). No matter
what obstacle is thrown my way: Report
from the single mothers' career readiness
and success project. The National College
Transition Network, World Education, ECMC
Foundation. http://www.collegetransition.org/
wp-content/uploads/2019/07/Full-Report-
NoMatter-What-Obstacle-July-2019.pdf

Johnson, S. (2019, August 21). Student debt rises
among the oldest borrowers. The Chronicle of
Higher Education.

Magnuson, K. (2007). Maternal Education
and children's academic achievement
during middle childhood. Developmental
Psychology, 43(6), 1497-1512. https://doi.
org/10.1037/0012-1649.43.6.1497

Miller, B. (2019, September 4). 3 ways federal
financial aid could work better for
student-parents. Center for American
Progress. https://www.americanprogress.
org/issues/educationpostsecondary/
news/2019/09/04/473930/3-ways-federal-
financial-aid-workbetter-student-parents/

Monaghan, D. (2016). Does college enrollment and bachelor's completion by mothers impact children's education outcomes? Sociology of Education, 90(1), 3-24. https://doi.org/10/1177/0038040716681054

Prickett, K. C. & Augustine, J. M. (2016). Maternal Education and Investments in Children's Health. Journal of Marriage and Family, 78(1), 7-25. doi:10.1111/jomf.12253

Reichlin Cruse, L., Gault, B., Suh, J., & DeMario, M. A. (2018). Time demands of single mother college students and the role of child care in their postsecondary success (Briefing Paper IWPR #C468). Institute for Women's Policy Research. https://iwpr.org/publications/single-mothers-college-time-use/UMN   SPHC – Academic Outcomes 38 | Wilder Research, May 2020

Reichlin Cruse, L., Holtzman, T., Gault, B., Croom, D., & Polk, P. (2019). Parents in college by the numbers. Institute for Women's Policy Research. https://iwpr.org/publications/parents-college-numbers/

Reichlin Cruse, L., Milli, J., Contreras-Mendez, S., Holtzman, T., & Gault, B. (2019). Investing in single mothers' Higher Education in Minnesota: Costs and benefits to individuals, families and society. Institute for Women's

Policy Research and Center on Equity in Higher Education. https://iwpr.org/wpcontent/uploads/2019/12/Minnesota.pdf

United States Government Accountability Office (GAO). (2019). Higher Education: More information could help student parents access additional federal student aid (Report to Congressional Requesters GAO-19-522). https://www.gao.gov/assets/710/701002.pdf

University of Minnesota. (n. d.). General College section of the 2004-2006 undergraduate catalog for the University of Minnesota,

Twin Cities campus. (n.d.). Retrieved February 3, 2020, from https://drive.google.com/drive/folders/1KufS-boaPR_JDdIdlkuPiXoeaK1zKITU

Zarifa, D., Kim, J., Seward, B., & Walters, D. (2018). What's taking you so long? Examining the effects of social class on completing a bachelor's degree in four years. Sociology of Education, 91(4), 290–322. https://doi.org/10.1177/0038040718802258

Pendleton, V & Atella, J. (2020). Academic Outcomes of Undergraduate Student Parents Served by the University of Minnesota's Student Parent Help Center. https://files.eric.ed.gov/fulltext/ED612480.pdf.